Preparing for your newborn

By
Kay Kavanagh

Preparing for your newborn
Copyright © 2009 by Kay Kavanagh
Kavanwood Publishing
All Rights Reserved.

No parts of this publication may be reproduced or used by any means, electronic or mechanical, including photocopying, without permission in writing from the Author.

The intent of the author is to provide an overview of what will be required for a newborn, but the listed items are not exhaustive, and no responsibility is taken for any items not listed.

Photographs on front cover taken by author.

www.lulu.com
Lulu Enterprises, Inc

ISBN: 978-0-9559939-0-9

First Edition

Dedicated to Sienna.

Contents

You're Pregnant! — 7
   Birth Plan — 9
   Hospital Bag — 12

Preparing Your Home — 18
   General home safety — 18
   In the kitchen — 19
   In the car — 20
   In the garden — 21

Getting Equipped! — 23
   Preparing the nursery — 23
   Sleeping — 24
   Changing — 25
   Clothing — 26
   Out and about — 27
   Extra's — 27
   Feeding — 28
   Bathing — 30
   Some non-essentials, but nice to have — 31

Preparing Your Finances — 33
After your baby is born — 35
Budget — 39
Notes: — 42

You're Pregnant!

Congratulations!

There are many items you will need to be ready for the birth of your newborn.

Follow the sections in this book to ensure you have covered all areas. This book has been designed in a way that you can 'tick off' each item as you obtain it, and thus keeps a track of all the items you still require.

This book is only a guideline, so blank spaces have been inserted for you to add you own extra items.

You have many things to think about whilst pregnant, so having this handy guide will hopefully help to keep things a little more organized!!

Birth Plan

Your midwife should discuss creating your birth plan with you, but you should consider the following, and remember that things don't always go to plan:

Where to give birth
- ☐ Hospital
- ☐ Home
- ☐ Midwife Unit

People
- ☐ Who will be your birth partner(s) (make sure you have their contact details on your birth plan)?
- ☐ If you want them there all the time, including if you have a caesarean?
- ☐ Are you happy for students to attend the birth?
- ☐ What role do you hope your midwife will take?

Equipment
- ☐ Any equipment you want to use: bean bags, birthing stools etc. and who will provide these.
- ☐ If you would like a water birth
- ☐ If you would like to have music playing during the labor
- ☐ If you will be using aromatherapy/herbal remedies/homeopathy during the labor
- ☐ Do you want to be able to eat and drink during labor?
- ☐ If you want foetal heart monitoring throughout labor.

Pain relief
- ☐ TENS Machine
- ☐ Gas and air
- ☐ Massage
- ☐ Spinal or epidural
- ☐ Pethidine

What position would you like for the labour and birth?
- ☐ Keeping mobile
- ☐ Lying, kneeling or squatting?

Delivery
- ☐ Would you rather have an episiotomy, or tear?
- ☐ Do you want to be told when to push or let your body guide you?
- ☐ Do you want to watch or feel the baby come out?
- ☐ If labor does not proceed do you want your waters broken?
- ☐ Do you wish to be induced?

When the baby is delivered
- ☐ Would you like the baby to be placed straight onto you're your tummy/breast, or cleaned up first?
- ☐ Would you like the sex announced?
- ☐ How you are planning to feed your new arrival, and if you would like some help.
- ☐ Who will cut the cord?
- ☐ How would you like to have the placenta delivered: with the aid of drugs, or naturally?

- ☐ Do you wish to keep the placenta?
- ☐ Do you want your baby to have a vitamin K injection?
- ☐ Do you want to stay in hospital few a couple of nights, or go home as soon as you can?

Caesarean

- ☐ What pain relief will you want should you need a caesarean?
- ☐ Would you like help holding your baby after having a caesarean?
- ☐ Would you like an elective caesarean?

Any special requirements

- ☐ Diet
- ☐ Disability
- ☐ Religious
- ☐ Do you wish to be cared for by women only?
- ☐ Do you need an interpreter?

Who should I give it to?

Keep your Birth Plan with your pregnancy notes, and take it with you to the hospital.

Your midwife can also look over it for you prior to labor, to ensure that you have covered all areas and to confirm that you have no further questions.

Hospital Bag

Regardless of where you are having your baby, you will need to put a few things aside, either at home for a home birth or in a hospital bag if you are having your baby in hospital. It's a good idea to have your hospital bag packed and ready about six weeks before your due date just in case your baby comes early. It can be useful to have more than 1 bag!

If you are traveling away from home, even for a day, you should take your hospital bag with you.

During labor:

- ☐ Your Maternity Notes.
- ☐ TENS Machine if you have opted for this type of pain relief.
- ☐ A watch with a second hand, to time your contractions.
- ☐ Bottled Water, Flannels, Water Spray & hand-held fan to keep you refreshed.
- ☐ A Mirror to watch your baby's head emerging!
- ☐ Massage Oil.
- ☐ Lip balm (your lips can become very dry during labor).
- ☐ Tissues.
- ☐ Warm socks, dressing gown and a large nightdress.
- ☐ Your birth plan.
- ☐ Hair bobble for long hair.
- ☐ Biscuits, Cereal or snack Bars, but check with your hospital that you are allowed these items first.
- ☐
- ☐
- ☐

It is important to remember that you may be required to stay in hospital overnight, or longer.

After baby is born – for you:

- ☐ Snacks & bottled water, especially if breastfeeding, as you can become very hungry.
- ☐ Disposable pants. You should take at least 6 pairs. Things can be a little messy post-birth!!
- ☐ Maternity Pads, at least 2 packs.
- ☐ Breast Pads & Nipple Cream – you may require these even if you are not planning on breastfeeding. Hormones run very high after giving birth, and you may find you leak milk regardless.
- ☐ Nursing Bras - at least 2 if planning on breastfeeding.
- ☐ Camera and spare batteries, to capture those precious moments.
- ☐ A book, pack of cards, mp3 player, travels games. These can help pass the time whilst your new baby is sleeping, however, you may be too tired, and need to sleep yourself.
- ☐ Shower gel, bubble bath, shampoo, conditioner, 2 hand towels and 2 bath towels. You may be able to have a bath following the birth.
- ☐ Hairbrush, deodorant, toothbrush/paste, make-up, soap & flannel.
- ☐ List of telephone numbers, mobile phone, or change to use hospital phones.
- ☐ 2 or 3 nightdresses (front-opening if you are planning on breastfeeding).
- ☐ Slippers (hospital floors can be cold!).

- ☐ Any medicine you are taking.
- ☐ 2 packets of tissues – you can be very hormonal after giving birth.
- ☐ Glasses / contact lenses.
- ☐ Change for the newspapers on the day your baby is born (to keep as a memento).
- ☐
- ☐
- ☐
- ☐
- ☐

After baby is born – for your new arrival:

- ☐ 1 pack of newborn diapers at least. It can also be worthwhile buying 2 sizes, in case your baby is larger or smaller than you though.
- ☐ Diaper bags.
- ☐ At least 6 cotton vests.
- ☐ At least 6 cotton sleep suits.
- ☐ Scratch mitts.
- ☐ Muslin Cloths (at least 6).
- ☐ Feeding equipment, depending upon your choice of feeding method.
- ☐ 3 Blankets.
- ☐ Diaper cream.
- ☐ Large bag of cotton wool.
- ☐ Baby wipes.
- ☐ Hat (especially for premature babies).
- ☐ Teddy or toy for the cot.
- ☐ Formula Milk of your choice: Make sure your choice of milk is also on your birth plan. Should your baby need to be taken to a Special Care Unit, they may need to know this information).
- ☐
- ☐
- ☐
- ☐
- ☐

For going home:
- ☐ Rear facing Car Seat if traveling by car.
- ☐ Outdoor clothes for you.
- ☐ Going home clothes for baby.
- ☐
- ☐
- ☐
- ☐
- ☐

Preparing Your Home

General home safety

- ☐ Get socket safety plugs for all the electricity plug sockets in your house and corner pads for any tables or furniture that your baby may hit their head on.
- ☐ Make sure all your smoke alarms are in good working order.
- ☐ Make sure you know how to operate everything in your home, especially all the new baby equipment.
- ☐ Get stair gates for both at the top and the bottom of every staircase.
- ☐ Keep a fire extinguisher in the house.
- ☐ Get some carbon monoxide detectors if you use gas or oil heating.
- ☐ Make sure you have a fully stocked first aid kit in your home.
- ☐ Put non-slip pads under all rugs.
- ☐ Start collecting vouchers/coupons. Baby items can be expensive, and every little helps!
- ☐ Make sure you have manual items to use, should you have a power cut i.e. cold-water sterilizer kits.
- ☐ Don't allow any of your pets into the room where your baby is sleeping. You can buy 'cat nets' which fit over the top of the cot to stop cats jumping in to 'get warm'!
- ☐ Keep medicine and all bathroom products away in a high cupboard.
- ☐ Fit a toilet seat lock.
- ☐ Put catches on all windows, or lock them.

- ☐ Fix safety catches and doorstoppers onto all cupboards and drawers.

In the kitchen

- ☐ Push everything to the back of kitchen worktops so that your baby cannot reach anything.
- ☐ Keep all chemicals and cleaning products out of reach and locked away.
- ☐ Cover your hob with a hob guard.
- ☐ If possible, turn the oven off at the mains each time you finish cooking.
- ☐ Get into the habit of always turning the saucepan & frying pan handles towards the back of the cooker.
- ☐ Stock up on Tea, Coffee, Sugar and milk, for all your guests after the birth.
- ☐ Try and make some homemade food in advance, and store it for when you don't have enough time.
- ☐ Stock up on tin food and soup for when you need a snack after the birth.
- ☐ Buy more Washing powder than you think you'll need – you'll be amazed how much washing one small baby can create!
- ☐
- ☐
- ☐
- ☐
- ☐

In the car

- ☐ Make sure you buy a rear-facing car seat, at least 6 weeks before your baby is due.
- ☐ If someone else is looking after your baby, ensure that they know how to fit the car seat properly.
- ☐ Never fix a car seat onto a seat that has an airbag.
- ☐ Fit sun visors on the window next to the car seat.
- ☐
- ☐
- ☐
- ☐
- ☐

In the garden

- ☐ Make sure your garden is secure and that your baby will not be able to crawl out. Check that all your gates fasten properly, and fix a lock to them if possible.

- ☐ Keep all garden tools and products safely locked away in a garage, shed or garden storage unit.

- ☐ Find out what all your plants are, and try to remove plants with berries or thorns.

- ☐ If you have a garden pond, make sure you have netting across the top so that your baby cannot accidentally fall in.

- ☐
- ☐
- ☐
- ☐
- ☐

Getting Equipped!

Preparing the nursery

There are some essential things to think about when preparing and designing the nursery:

- Will the furniture grow with your child, or are you happy to replace the furniture as they grow?
- Is the furniture durable, and child-friendly?
- Do you want to decorate or accessorize with a theme?
- Can you fit a dimmer switch to limit the glare of the light bulb for nighttime feeds?
- Can the cot be placed away from any radiators, heaters and direct sunlight?

Sleeping

Make sure you wash all bedding prior to your baby coming home.

- ☐ Baby monitor
- ☐ Cot bumpers. These can keep away draughts and protect your baby from hurting themselves on the bars.
- ☐ Cot, Cot Bed, Crib or Moses Basket. Think about where your baby is going to sleep and what type of unit will fit in each area. Also consider the length of time each unit can be used for before your baby will outgrow it.
- ☐ Mattress, 4 fitted sheets, 4 Top sheets, 4 Blankets (for all bed types to be used).
- ☐ 4 sleeping bags. Sleeping bags are a convenient option over the use of blankets, as you use a sleeping bag to match the room temperature. In the early days, you can also feed your baby whilst they are in the sleeping bag, which helps when you but your baby back to bed, as their temperature stays constant.
- ☐ You may want to fit blackout blinds and insect nets over the windows in all the rooms that will be used by the baby.
- ☐ Night-light. Please note that these do not generally provide enough light for you to work by, and extra lighting will be required at night for feeding/changing times.
- ☐ Room thermometer.
- ☐ 6-8 sleep suits and vests.
- ☐
- ☐
- ☐
- ☐

Changing

- ☐ Waterproof Changing Mat.
- ☐ Diaper Cream.
- ☐ Cotton Wool.
- ☐ Top & Tail bowl.
- ☐ Baby wipes.
- ☐ Laundry bag.
- ☐ Diapers.
- ☐ If using washable diapers: diaper liners, diaper covers and sterilising fluid.
- ☐ Diaper bin.
- ☐ Changing unit. It is more convenient to have changing areas both up and downstairs if possible.
- ☐
- ☐
- ☐
- ☐
- ☐

Clothing

Make sure you wash all clothing prior to your baby coming home.

- ☐ 2 Hats – more for premature babies.
- ☐ 6-8 cotton vests.
- ☐ 2 cardigans or jumpers.
- ☐ 4-6 Day outfits.
- ☐ 2-3 pairs of cotton socks.
- ☐ Slip on bootees or pram shoes.
- ☐ 2-3 Shawls.
- ☐ 1 Jacket or coat.
- ☐ 6-8 cotton stretch suits.
- ☐ 2 pairs of Scratch mittens.
- ☐ Non-Biological washing powder.
- ☐
- ☐
- ☐
- ☐
- ☐

Out and about

- ☐ Car seat.
- ☐ Window blinds.
- ☐ Baby rear view mirror.
- ☐ Stroller, Travel System or newborn buggy / pushchair – think about size and options available.
- ☐ Rain covers.
- ☐ Baby carrier or sling. Be aware that some of these require your baby to be of a minimum weight.
- ☐ Changing Bag.
- ☐
- ☐
- ☐
- ☐
- ☐

Extra's

- ☐ 6 x pacifiers.
- ☐ Breathing monitor / alarm.
- ☐
- ☐
- ☐
- ☐
- ☐

Feeding

If Bottle Feeding:

- ☐ Muslin Squares.
- ☐ 6 Bibs.
- ☐ 6 Bottles, with teats and lids. Buy different sized teats in case your baby requires a bigger/smaller size.
- ☐ Sterilising Unit or Kit.
- ☐ Bottle & Teat brush.
- ☐ Dried baby formula milk.
- ☐ Milk bottle thermometer.
- ☐ Night feeding unit. You can get units that assist with night feeds, by keeping water cool and having a heating option.
- ☐ Consider a thermal bottle jacket, flask and ice pack options for feeding when out and about.
- ☐
- ☐
- ☐
- ☐
- ☐

If Breastfeeding:

- ☐ Muslin Squares.
- ☐ 6 Bibs.
- ☐ Nursing Bra's (at least 3).
- ☐ Breast pump.
- ☐ Nipple shields.
- ☐ Milk storage bags for freezing.
- ☐ Sterilising Equipment.
- ☐ Milk bottle thermometer.
- ☐ Gel nursing pads.
- ☐ Pack of Breast Pads.
- ☐ Nursing pillow and/or chair.
- ☐
- ☐
- ☐
- ☐
- ☐

Bathing

- ☐ Baby bath or 'top & tail' bowl.
- ☐ Cotton wool balls.
- ☐ 2 soft sponges or flannels.
- ☐ Baby liquid soap/shampoo.
- ☐ 2 baby towels with hoods.
- ☐ Bath thermometer.
- ☐ Baby lotion or oil.
- ☐ Baby talc.
- ☐ Brush & comb.
- ☐ Baby nail scissors.
- ☐ Baby First Aid Kit / Medical Kit.
- ☐
- ☐
- ☐
- ☐
- ☐

Some non-essentials, but nice to have

- ☐ Activity Play mat (Waterproof or washable).
- ☐ Height chart for the nursery.
- ☐ Decorations for the nursery.
- ☐ Back and Head support (you can get ones to prevent 'flathead' syndrome).
- ☐ Baby view car mirror so that you can see your baby in the car seat.
- ☐ Breathing monitor.
- ☐ Cot mobile.
- ☐ Bouncing cradle or swing.
- ☐ 2 soft rattles.
- ☐ Nursing chair.
- ☐ Travel cot.
- ☐
- ☐
- ☐
- ☐
- ☐

Preparing Your Finances

Mortgage
- Ensure that your mortgage is on the most competitive rate. Some mortgage companies will also allow a 'payment holiday' when you have a baby.

Insurance
- Make sure that all your insurance policies are up to date and have a competitive price, including Life Cover.

Household bills
- Compare your utilities suppliers to make sure you are on the best deal. Most will also offer discounts for paying by direct debit.

Make a Will
- Make a Will, using a solicitor if needed.

Benefits
- Ensure to investigate what benefits you will be entitled to once your baby has been born, and make sure you know how to apply for them.

Nursery Fees / Childcare
- It is worth investigating local options for Nurseries and Childcare, should you be planning on returning to work. Often these can have waiting lists, and the costs will also need to be factored into your budget.

After your baby is born

There are various items that you may wish to purchase now, for after your baby is born.

Baby Book
- There are many baby books available for you to record all your baby's events from birth, through their first year. They make a great 'keepsake' to look back on in years to come.

Baby Memento box (or Memories Box)
- You might like to make or buy a box to use to store all the baby's mementos, from birth and throughout their younger years.

  A benefit to having this prior to your baby being born is that you can also save mementos from your pregnancy, as you progress through the 9 months.

Baby Website & Blog
- Why not set-up a website for your baby? There are numerous websites online that you can use.

  You can set-up a Blog online, and keep a diary of how your little one is progressing, and what they're getting up to each day – you can then share this with your friends and family.

Gifts
- There are various websites offering a free 'Gift List' service. They are ideal to add all the items that you still require onto, and you can give the list details to friends and family, either before or after the birth, or for future Birthdays and Christmas.

Baby Sign language

- Baby sign language is becoming very popular, as it has been proved that you can communicate with your baby faster than waiting for them to talk.

  Buy books or tools now, so that you have them ready for when your baby can start to understand. It is said that the earlier you start to communicate to your baby, using sign language as well as talking, the more beneficial it will be.

Get organized (again!)

- Buy a family calendar (even the baby will have Appointments!)
- Shop for your groceries online
- Stock up on Birthday cards
- Cook more food than you need when you have extra time, then freeze the extra for when you have less time.
- Try to get a routine
- Most importantly, enjoy time with your new baby!

Track your gifts

When your baby is born you will no doubt receive numerous gifts and cards. It is a good idea to track gifts, so that you can send 'Thank You' cards:

Who gift was from	Gift Description	Thank-You card sent?

Budget

Item	Estimated Cost	Actual Cost

Item	Estimated Cost	Actual Cost

Item	Estimated Cost	Actual Cost

Notes:

www.ingramcontent.com/pod-product-compliance
Ingram Content Group UK Ltd.
Pitfield, Milton Keynes, MK11 3LW, UK
UKHW041433180426
11947UKWH00007B/412